31 DAYS
OF
Prayer
FOR
Caregivers

This Journal Belongs to:

_____

VISIT:

WWW.CAREGIVINGGRACEFULLY.COM

FOR TIPS, FREE TOOLS, AND MORE.

A CAREGIVER'S PRAYER

DAY 1

Heavenly Father, Most High God, I rejoice in You. My heart is filled with thanksgiving. You have entrusted and equipped me for awesome work as a caregiver. You knew before I was knitted in my mother's womb that I would be given this assignment, this good work. Thank you for entrusting me with this great task. I consider it an honor that you have hand-selected me. Thank you for the time you have given me to enjoy with my loved one. I'm grateful for the times we share, no matter how challenging they can be at times. I praise you for giving me the perfect example in your son, Jesus Christ. Help me as I strive to emulate His character.

Lord, while I come with a heart full of thanksgiving and praise, I also come before you humbly with a repentant heart. Forgive me for all the times I have grumbled and complained out of frustration, fear, and fatigue. Forgive me for any resentment I harbor against those who look and

judge and offer opinions but do not offer to help. Quiet my mouth and spirit when I want to respond in an ungodly manner. Give me a spirit to forgive freely. Remove any bitterness I have regarding my current situation.

A CAREGIVER'S PRAYER CONTINUED...

DAY 1

Take away my "why me spirit." I know you are no respecter of persons. You are sovereign and Your will is perfect. I also know that all things work together for the good of those who love God. So, today I turn away from my selfish ways and negative spirit. I crucify my flesh and I choose you.

Lord, quiet my spirit before you. Help me call in my wandering thoughts and be still in your presence so that I can hear you more clearly, with my ears and my heart. Tear down the walls I have built around myself. Make my heart tender again. I yield to your will and your way. I surrender to your lordship. Align my will with your will.

Lord, you told me that if I come to you with my prayers and petitions, that you would give peace that surpasses all understanding (Philippians 4:7). I come seeking that peace. Nudge me daily, reminding me to acknowledge you. Show me your presence even in the small things. Help me crave time spent with you. Refresh and renew me in those quiet moments spent with you. Lord, I pray for strength to endure this journey. Help me rise every day, energized and ready to take on the challenges that come.

A CAREGIVER'S PRAYER CONTINUED...

DAY 1

Give me mental clarity to think critically when necessary, help me be creative when new challenges arise, and give me a compassionate heart to love unconditionally. Show me the blessing in every situation. Some days are harder than others, but what remains consistent is my dependence on you. When I am weak, your strength is made perfect (II Corinthians 12:9-10). Only you can cause me to run, but not grow weary, walk but not faint (Isaiah 40:31). Only you can keep me from stumbling (Jude 1).

When I am afraid, remind me that you did not give me the spirit of fear, but rather power, love, and a sound mind (2 Timothy 1:7). When I am tired, give me sweet rest. When I am lonely, be my friend. When I cannot find the words, Holy Spirit please intercede for me (Romans 8:26-27). Renew me day by day, showering me with new mercies. Give me the patience I need when caring for _____. Remind me of the patience you have with me and the loving-kindness you show me continuously. I'm asking for a double portion of the fruits of the spirit when caring for _____, love, joy, peace, patience, goodness, kindness, faithfulness, gentleness, and self-control.

Lord, I ask these blessings in the name of your precious son, Jesus. Amen.

A CAREGIVER'S PRAYER

DAY 1

_____
_____
_____
_____
_____
_____
_____
_____
_____
_____
_____
_____
_____

LIST OF GRATITUDE

_____
_____
_____
_____
_____

ANSWERED PRAYERS

_____
_____
_____
_____
_____
_____
_____
_____

FRUITS OF THE *Spirit*

LOVE

DAY 2

Thank you Lord, for showing us what agape love is. Love that knows no limits. It's radical and selfless, and thankfully for me, unstoppable. In fact, the Bible tells me, you are Love and that "There is no fear in love. But perfect love drives out fear because fear has to do with punishment. The one who fears is not made perfect in love. We love because he first loved us." So, if you are love and I am created in your own image, help me pour out that incomprehensible fearless love all over my loved one today. We ask these blessings in Jesus' name. Amen.

I JOHN 4:18-19

LOVE

DAY 2

_____
_____
_____
_____
_____
_____
_____
_____
_____
_____
_____
_____
_____
_____
_____
_____
_____
_____
_____
_____

LIST OF GRATITUDE

_____
_____
_____
_____
_____
_____

ANSWERED PRAYERS

_____
_____
_____
_____
_____
_____

JOY

DAY 3

Lord, I'm in need of a dose of good medicine this morning. Your word says a "joyful heart is good medicine, but a crushed spirit dries up the bones." Fill my heart with joy today. Show me joy in the small things in the quiet moments. Reveal it to me in moments of frustration, anxiety, and sadness. Help me to rejoice in all things, especially you. We know weeping may endure for a night, But joy comes in the morning. We ask these blessings in Jesus' name. Amen.

PROVERBS 17:22, PSALMS 30:5

JOY

DAY 3

LIST OF GRATITUDE

ANSWERED PRAYERS

PEACE

DAY 4

Heavenly Father, I come to you with thanksgiving this morning regardless of my circumstances or feelings. I'm casting my cares on you this morning, because I know that your word says to, "Be anxious for nothing, but in everything by prayer and supplication, with thanksgiving, let your requests be made known to God; and the peace of God, which surpasses all understanding, will guard your hearts and minds through Christ Jesus." I want that peace today, so I intentionally call out to you in prayer this morning, with thanksgiving and making my petitions know to you. I gladly thank you for your son, Jesus, and the gift of salvation. I thank you for another day to rise. I thank you for mental clarity, health and strength. I thank you for my loved one and for giving me the ability to care for him/her. Help me worry less and cherish more. In Jesus' name, I pray. Amen.

PHILIPPIANS 4:6-7

PEACE

DAY 4

_____

LIST OF GRATITUDE

_____

ANSWERED PRAYERS

_____

PATIENCE

DAY 5

Lord, thank you for today. Thank you for being a supernatural God, who imparts your supernatural power to me through your Holy Spirit. Lord, I struggle with patience sometimes, but today I leave impatience at the door. I'm asking you for a double portion of supernatural spiritual fruit, and that fruit is patience. Whenever I feel impatience rising, help me remember to stop, take a deep breath, and intentionally choose patience over frustration. Give me the patience to listen to my loved one and hear. Give me the patience to see his/her deeper needs and to serve. Finally, give me the patience to see the love of Christ in him/her and love unconditionally. We ask these blessings in Jesus' name. Amen.

ROMANS 12:12

PATIENCE

DAY 5

_____

_____

_____

_____

_____

_____

_____

_____

_____

_____

_____

_____

_____

_____

_____

LIST OF GRATITUDE

_____

_____

_____

_____

_____

_____

ANSWERED PRAYERS

_____

_____

_____

_____

_____

_____

KINDNESS

Loving Father, thank you for the kindness you show me daily in every area of my life. Enable me to show kindness to others in the same way. I want my kindness to be a direct reflection of you and the agape love you shower me with, not the kind or not so kind things people do to me or others. Help me remove the conditions. I want to show outrageous, incomprehensible kindness to my loved ones and others, so I ask you for a double portion of the spiritual fruit of kindness. May my kindness tree be heavy with spiritual fruit. These blessings I ask in the loving name of Jesus. Amen.

COLOSSIANS 3:12, PROVERBS
21:21

KINDNESS

DAY 6

LIST OF GRATITUDE

ANSWERED PRAYERS

GOODNESS

Loving God, thank you for your goodness. We know all good things come from you. You are the source. In your generosity, you created me in your own likeness, therefore goodness is intrinsically in me. My flesh is also with me. Help me arise and choose you daily. I choose goodness. Empower me to crucify my flesh daily, along with anything else that is not like you. Cause me to reflect the Character of Christ in all things, but especially in caring for my loved one. Help me sacrifice myself in selfless service as I gracefully provide care. I ask these blessings of goodness in Jesus' name. Amen.

.

GALATIANS 6:10, EPHESIANS 4:29

GOODNESS

DAY 7

_____
_____
_____
_____
_____
_____
_____
_____
_____
_____
_____
_____
_____
_____
_____

LIST OF GRATITUDE

_____
_____
_____
_____
_____
_____
_____

ANSWERED PRAYERS

_____
_____
_____
_____
_____
_____

FAITHFULNESS

Father God, thank you for your commitment and faithfulness to me. You are the perfect example of what I should strive to be. You have hand-selected me for this task of caregiving and it's not always easy, but I trust that you have well equipped me for this good work. When I grow weary, remind me of your unwavering faithfulness. Cause my mind to go back and remind me of why I started this journey. Refresh my desire to give care gracefully. I rebuke any spirits of uncertainty, fear, or selfishness. Help me stay the course and follow your lead. Your will is perfect. In Jesus' name. Amen.

MATTHEW 25:21

FAITHFULNESS

DAY 8

_____

_____

_____

_____

_____

_____

_____

_____

_____

_____

_____

_____

_____

_____

_____

_____

LIST OF GRATITUDE

_____

_____

_____

_____

_____

_____

ANSWERED PRAYERS

_____

_____

_____

_____

_____

_____

GENTLENESS

DAY 9

Lord, thank you for the fruit of gentleness. Cultivate this fruit in me. Help me to be gentle in both action and word. The Bible says, "A gentle tongue is a tree of life, but perverseness in it breaks the spirit." I want to be a tree of life in my home, showering my loved ones with gentleness. When frustration rises up in me, please remind me of how gentle you are with me. In the lovely name of Jesus. Amen.

PROVERBS 15:4

GENTLNESS

DAY 9

_____
_____
_____
_____
_____
_____
_____
_____
_____
_____
_____
_____
_____
_____
_____
_____
_____
_____

LIST OF GRATITUDE

_____
_____
_____
_____
_____
_____

ANSWERED PRAYERS

_____
_____
_____
_____
_____
_____

SELF-CONTROL

DAY 10

Gracious God, thank you for the gift of a sound mind. Your word says, "A man without self-control is like a city broken into and left without walls." Help me exhibit self-control and restraint in all that I do, but especially in my caregiving efforts. Help me reign in my thoughts, words, and actions. Cause me to listen before I react, being slow to speak and slow to anger. Keep me from any addictive behaviors as a means to cope with the stress of caregiving. Remind me to consult you first in all things. In Jesus' name, I pray. Amen.

PROVERBS 25:28

SELF-CONTROL

DAY 10

_____
_____
_____
_____
_____
_____
_____
_____
_____
_____
_____
_____
_____
_____
_____
_____
_____
_____

LIST OF GRATITUDE

_____

_____

_____

_____

_____

_____

_____

ANSWERED PRAYERS

_____

_____

_____

_____

_____

_____

_____

SELF
Care

FEAR

DAY 11

Abba Father, thank you for being my rock in a weary land. This caregiver journey is more difficult than I ever could have imagined and I get afraid sometimes. Lord, remind me in my times of fear that you did not give me a spirit of fear, but of power and of love and of a sound mind. You love me and your love is absolutely perfect and your word reminds me that perfect love casts out fear. It must flee in your presence. Thank you for your perfect love and your Holy Spirit that comforts me. In the matchless name of Jesus. Amen.

II TIMOTHY 1:7

FEAR

DAY 11

_____

_____

_____

_____

_____

_____

_____

_____

_____

_____

_____

_____

_____

_____

_____

_____

_____

_____

_____

LIST OF GRATITUDE

_____

_____

_____

_____

_____

_____

_____

ANSWERED PRAYERS

_____

_____

_____

_____

_____

_____

_____

DEPRESSION

DAY 12

Abba Father, thank you for your plan for my life. I know that everything I am going through right now, you knew about before the being of time. I know that you have a plan to prosper me, not harm me. All of these things that are happening right now, are happening for my good because I love you. So, I rebuke the spirit of depression right now in the name of Jesus. Depression has no place in my life. I am walking in my divine destiny. All feelings of inadequacy, insecurity, and sadness must flee, in the name of Jesus. Weeping may endure for a night, but Joy comes in the morning. Lord, dry my tears and cause me to rejoice as only you can. I choose joy today, in Jesus' name. Amen.

PSALMS 30:5

DEPRESSION

DAY 12

_____

_____

_____

_____

_____

_____

_____

_____

_____

_____

_____

_____

_____

_____

_____

_____

_____

LIST OF GRATITUDE

_____

_____

_____

_____

_____

_____

_____

ANSWERED PRAYERS

_____

_____

_____

_____

_____

_____

_____

ISOLATION

Heavenly Father, thank you for your friendship. You are closer than any brother or mother. You are my best friend when I feel like I'm all alone. But Lord, you have also created relationships and community for a reason. You have given us the body of Christ to remain in fellowship with others. As a caregiver, I feel myself drifting further and further from others, even my family sometimes. I know you didn't give me this selfless assignment, pulling me outside of myself, to separate me from others. I reject any feelings of isolation and I seek fellowship. I ask that you send someone in the moments when I feel most isolated, to visit, call, or text, to let me know you hear my cries. Remind me to reach out to others also. Strengthen my bonds with friends and family during this challenging season. In Jesus' name, I pray. Amen.

ECCLESIASTES 4:9-10

ISOLATION

DAY 13

_____
_____
_____
_____
_____
_____
_____
_____
_____
_____
_____
_____
_____

LIST OF GRATITUDE

_____

_____

_____

_____

_____

_____

ANSWERED PRAYERS

_____

_____

_____

_____

_____

_____

STRESS

Heavenly Father, thank you for being a burden bearer. Remind me to take on your yoke. I know your yoke is easy, but sometimes I forget and I take so much stress on myself. Help me break that cycle. Lord, allow me to lay my burdens at your feet and leave them there. Your word tells me that if I make my petitions to you that you will give me your peace, and your peace is incomprehensible. A peace like no other. I trade in my stress for peace today. In Jesus' name. Amen.

MATTHEW 11:28-30

STRESS

DAY 14

LIST OF GRATITUDE

ANSWERED PRAYERS

RESENTMENT

Heavenly Father, cleanse me today. Your word tells me to "Let all bitterness, wrath, anger, clamor, and evil speaking be put away from me, with all malice. And be kind to one another, tenderhearted, forgiving one another, even as God in Christ forgave me." But sometimes it's hard to let go, Lord. Sometimes I wonder why you have charged me with this enormous task of being a caregiver, while others freely live their lives? Why have you afflicted my loved one in this way? When these questions overwhelm me, remind me of your sovereignty and your perfect will. I know your word promises that all things work together for the good of those who love you. This is ALL THINGS, so resentment and unforgiveness, flee from me, in the Mighty name of Jesus. Amen!

EPHESIANS 4:31-32

RESENTMENT

DAY 15

LIST OF GRATITUDE

ANSWERED PRAYERS

SURRENDER

Heavenly Father, Thank you for sitting on the throne. Thank you for Lordship in my life. Thank you for choosing me. Thank you for saving me, for that I am eternally grateful. Lord, forgive me for all the days I arise unsurrendered, operating in my flesh and thinking I'm using my own power. Making foolish things idols in my life. Help me wake up daily and choose to turn away from that lifestyle and turn to you. I SURRENDER in the matchless name of Jesus. Amen.

ROMANS 12:1

SURRENDER

DAY 16

_____
_____
_____
_____
_____
_____
_____
_____
_____
_____
_____
_____

LIST OF GRATITUDE

_____
_____
_____
_____
_____
_____

ANSWERED PRAYERS

_____
_____
_____
_____
_____
_____

IDOLS

Lord, thank you for being the one and true living God. Holy, Holy, Holy is your name. Lord, I come to you with a repentant heart. Forgive me for anything or one I have made an idol and put before you. Please, help me turn my heart towards you and away from temporal things. If I am making an idol out of my loved one, I ask that you open my eyes so that I don't think of him/her more highly than I should, while still honoring and caring for them gracefully. If there is a physical thing or thought that I am idolizing, Lord, remove it. I surrender to your Lordship, you must reign supreme in my life. I humble myself before you. May you extract glory from every area of my life. In the mighty name of Jesus, I pray. Amen.

EXODUS 20:3-6

IDOLS

DAY 17

_____
_____
_____
_____
_____
_____
_____
_____
_____
_____
_____
_____
_____
_____
_____
_____
_____

LIST OF GRATITUDE

_____

_____

_____

_____

_____

_____

_____

ANSWERED PRAYERS

_____

_____

_____

_____

_____

_____

_____

WEAKNESS

Lord, thank you for my weakness today.
Some days I feel so weak, from the stress
and strain of being a caregiver, but I am
reminded that your word says in my
weakness, your strength is made perfect.
So, I'm thankful to you for my weakness,
that is swallowed up by your strength. I am
in awe of your power and strength. Your
strength is unmatched. So, I rest today in my
weakness and relinquish all to you. In Jesus'
name, I pray. Amen.

II CORINTHIANS 12:9-10

WEAKNESS

DAY 18

LIST OF GRATITUDE

ANSWERED PRAYERS

SELFISHNESS

Lord, thank you for your generosity. You are my example in every area of life, because your selflessness, constant sacrifice, and long-suffering constantly humble me. Lord, I repent of my selfish ways. Please righteously convict me, when selfishness overtakes me. It's not Christ-Like and I need a transformation. Remind me of your selfless ways. Help me crucify my flesh when my selfish ways rise up. Renew my mind in this area. Create in me a clean heart. These things I ask in Jesus's name. Amen.

PHILIPPIANS 2:4,
I CORINTHIANS 10:24

SELFISHNESS

DAY 19

_____
_____
_____
_____
_____
_____
_____
_____
_____
_____
_____
_____

LIST OF GRATITUDE

_____
_____
_____
_____
_____
_____

ANSWERED PRAYERS

_____
_____
_____
_____
_____
_____

SELF-CARE

Father God, thank you for giving me my body, your temple. Remind me to care for it with tenderness. No one mistreats or abuses borrowed things, so remind me that my body is not my own it's yours. Help me be more mindful of the types and amounts of food I put into. Remind me to hydrate myself regularly. Show when I need rest and renewal. Above all, make me conscious of what I allow into mind, with what I see, hear, and engage in. Allow me to present myself as a living sacrifice for your glory. In Christ's name. Amen.

I CORINTHIANS 6:19-20,
ROMANS 12:1

SELF-CARE

DAY 20

LIST OF GRATITUDE

ANSWERED PRAYERS

HEALTH

Lord, thank you for my health. I ask that you continue to sustain me as I care for my loved one. I ask that you heal me in areas of my body that are or may be compromised. By your stripes I am healed. Remind me to care for my body. Help me choose good things to nourish it and convict me when I don't feel like staying active. My body is your temple. I want to be intentional in caring for this beautiful gift you have given me. Strengthen me Lord, not just in physical health, but in mental and spiritual health as well. I ask these blessings of health in Jesus' name. Amen.

I CORINTHIANS 6:19

HEALTH

DAY 21

_____
_____
_____
_____
_____
_____
_____
_____
_____
_____
_____
_____

LIST OF GRATITUDE

_____
_____
_____
_____
_____
_____
_____

ANSWERED PRAYERS

_____
_____
_____
_____
_____
_____
_____

GIFTS FROM
God

GRACE

DAY 22

Lord, thank you for the gift of grace. You give it so freely and for that, I'm grateful. I'm so grateful that I humbly ask you for more. Grant me grace as I adjust and readjust to our ever-changing lives. Grant me grace as I learn to manage new medical conditions that arise for my loved one. Please, grant me grace when I struggle with accepting the hard sacrifices I'm faced with as a caregiver. I know my circumstances are challenging, but your grace is sufficient. May your grace be sufficient in my life today. Jesus' name, I pray. Amen.

EPHESIANS 4:7

GRACE

DAY 22

LIST OF GRATITUDE

ANSWERED PRAYERS

MERCY

Lord, thank you for a brand new day, full of new mercies promised in your word. Please, shower me with new mercies today, as I care for my loved one. Some days I'm mad, sad, frustrated. Some days I'm downright angry. I thank you for not allowing these feelings to consume me. I don't always get it right, but thankfully you have gifted me brand new mercies every morning. So, I arise today, joyful, grateful, and renewed, because of your mercies. I ask that you continue to renew my mind today. In Jesus' name. Amen.

LAMENTATIONS 3:22-23,
HEBREWS 4:16

MERCY

DAY 23

_____

_____

_____

_____

_____

_____

_____

_____

_____

_____

_____

_____

LIST OF GRATITUDE

_____

_____

_____

_____

_____

_____

ANSWERED PRAYERS

_____

_____

_____

_____

_____

_____

TIME WITH GOD

DAY 24

Abba Father, hallowed be thy name. Thank you for being a good father. I come to you, humbly seeking your face. Help me chase after you more and more. Cause me to crave being in your presence. Call my wandering thoughts under your submission. Cause me to hunger for your word, chewing on it constantly. Show me how to thirst after intimacy with you. Make your countenance shine upon me. Reveal yourself to me. Expose the Christ in me, so that I may be closer to you and show Christ to others. In Jesus' name. Amen.

JOHN 15:5, MATTHEW 7:7

TIME WITH GOD

DAY 24

_____

_____

_____

_____

_____

_____

_____

_____

_____

_____

_____

_____

LIST OF GRATITUDE

_____

_____

_____

_____

_____

_____

ANSWERED PRAYERS

_____

_____

_____

_____

_____

_____

WISDOM

DAY 25

Heavenly Father, in the name of Jesus, I thank you for the gift of wisdom. Your word says this is a gift that you give freely to those who ask. I come asking for wisdom today. Help me consult you in all things. Give me the wisdom to care for my loved one confidently. Your word says when I walk, my steps will not be hindered, And when I run, I will not stumble if I walk according to wisdom. Help me seek wise counsel when necessary. Allow me to discern unwise counsel. Give me peace in my decision-making. I humbly submit to your will and your way, because the fear of you is the beginning of all understanding. I ask these blessings in the matchless name of Jesus. Amen.

PROVERBS 1, PROVERBS 4:12

WISDOM

DAY 25

_____
_____
_____
_____
_____
_____
_____
_____
_____
_____
_____
_____
_____

LIST OF GRATITUDE

_____
_____
_____
_____
_____
_____
_____

ANSWERED PRAYERS

_____
_____
_____
_____
_____
_____
_____

REST

Lord, thank you for sweet rest. Jesus said in your word, "Come to Me, all you who labor and are heavy laden, and I will give you rest." While caring for my loved one is a labor of love, it is labor no less, and I am heavy-ladened by the many tasks and responsibilities each day brings. Sometimes it feels like It Is more than I can mentally and physically handle. But thank you for being a burden bearer and a heavy load sharer. I drop my burdens at your feet this morning as I go about my day, trusting that will give me rest at just the right moments and never put more on me than I can bear. I need only ask. Help me rest in your perfect will today. In Jesus' name, I pray. Amen.

ISAIAH 14:3, MATTHEW 11:58

REST

DAY 26

LIST OF GRATITUDE

ANSWERED PRAYERS

RENEWAL

DAY 27

Thank you, Lord, for your renewal. I sing with the psalmist, "Create in me a pure heart, O God, and renew a steadfast spirit within me. Do not cast me from your presence or take your Holy Spirit from me. Restore to me the joy of your salvation and grant me a willing spirit, to sustain me." I declare that I am renewed and refreshed, ready to reflect the love of Christ in my care today. I am a willing vessel, fill me up so that I may be a blessing to my loved one today. These blessings I ask in Jesus' name. Amen.

PSALM 51:10-12, ISAIAH 40:31

RENEWAL

DAY 27

_____
_____
_____
_____
_____
_____
_____
_____
_____
_____
_____

LIST OF GRATITUDE

_____
_____
_____
_____
_____
_____

ANSWERED PRAYERS

_____
_____
_____
_____
_____
_____

ENDURANCE

DAY 28

Lord thank you for another day. Please help me endure this race. This road as a caregiver is rough and I get tired sometimes, but Your word says, "To those who by persistence in doing good seek glory, honor, and immortality, he will give eternal life." Lord, help me stay the course. I may stumble, but I will not fall, for you the Lord upholds me. Jesus' name, I pray. Amen.

ROMANS 2:7, PSALMS 37:24

ENDURANCE

DAY 28

_____
_____
_____
_____
_____
_____
_____
_____
_____
_____
_____
_____
_____
_____

LIST OF GRATITUDE

_____

_____

_____

_____

_____

ANSWERED PRAYERS

_____

_____

_____

_____

_____

PRODUCTIVITY

DAY 29

Lord, thank you for this brand new day, another chance to accomplish things that need to be done. I will not eat the bread of idleness. My hands are strong for my task. Give me focus and mental clarity to focus on things that are most important and prioritize properly. Remove the spirit of procrastination from me. Let me know the perfect times to rest and when to get up and go. Refresh me, energize me, motivate me. Help me keep my eyes on my goals, but never make idols out of them. You are the Lord of my life. With you, I know I can accomplish much. Lord, these and other blessings I ask in Jesus' name. Amen.

PROVERBS 31:17, 27

PRODUCTIVITY

DAY 29

LIST OF GRATITUDE

ANSWERED PRAYERS

GRIEF

Abba Father, thank you for the time I have left with my loved one. Help me to cherish this time. But Lord, I am also asking you for comfort during this season. I am grieving, Lord, and my heart is broken. Grieving the loss of the way my loved one used to be. He/she is just a shell of who he/she once was. I long for our old relationship and the times we shared. Mend my broken heart, Lord. I know To most people on the outside, looking in, they don't understand and can't relate, so I'm asking that you send me other people who understand and who can support me. I am bringing this petition to you with great expectations because I am in need of comfort, grace, and understanding. Holy Spirit, Great Comforter, dry my eyes and lift up my bowed down head. Please, remind me of what I have right in front of me. I know you are faithful to do just as I ask. In Jesus' name, I pray. Amen.

MATTHEW 5:4

GRIEF

DAY 30

_____

_____

_____

_____

_____

_____

_____

_____

_____

_____

_____

_____

_____

_____

_____

_____

LIST OF GRATITUDE

_____

_____

_____

_____

_____

_____

ANSWERED PRAYERS

_____

_____

_____

_____

_____

_____

HELP

DAY 31

Father God, thank you for co-laborers. I pray that as you strengthen and encourage me on this journey, that you also encourage them. Remind them that you chose them for a reason. Refresh and renew them regularly. Cause us to be on one accord in our joint efforts in caregiving. Remind us both to seek your counsel. Help us support one another and be a comfort to one another as we go through the ups and downs of this journey. Bless them in Jesus' name. Amen.

ECCLESIASTES 4:9-10

HELP

DAY 31

LIST OF GRATITUDE

ANSWERED PRAYERS

Made in the USA
Coppell, TX
20 December 2024

43215012R00079